I can make Angel things for Christmas

Crafts by Jocelyn Miller

Photography by John Williams

Illustration by Adrian Barclay

Contents

1 The angel and the lily

The Christmas story is about a birth. It begins when the angel Gabriel visits Mary and tells her she will have a baby: God's Son, Jesus. The story is found in the Bible.

  For hundreds of years, many artists who have imagined this scene have shown the angel giving Mary a lily.

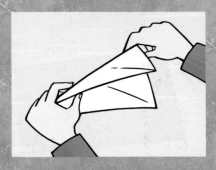

1 Take a square of paper in your chosen colour. A piece 20cm x 20cm is easy to work with. Fold corner to corner, then crease and uncrease on both diagonals so the creases form valleys.

2 Turn the paper over so the valleys becomes ridges. Fold side to side, crease and uncrease; fold top to bottom, crease and uncrease. Now lower to corners and let the paper fold squeeze into the shape shown. Think of four petal shapes: 1 opposite 3 and 2 opposite 4.

3 Take one triangular petal flap and squash into a kite shape. Turn the piece over and repeat for petal flap 3. Then turn a flap like a book and repeat for petal flaps 2 and 4.

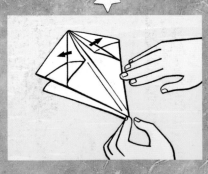

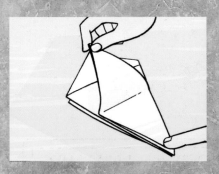

4 Place the shape with the folded point towards you. Now fold the top edges of one petal to meet in the centre as shown. Unfold.

5 Fold the top point to the bottom point through all layers, crease and unfold. Next, pull down the topmost point and watch the sides come to the middle. Press flat.

6 Fold the triangular flap in the centre up. Turn the paper and repeat steps 4 and 5 with petal flap 3; then open like a book and repeat with petal flaps 2 and 4.

7 You have a diamond shape like this.

8 Still with the folded point towards you, fold the bottom sides of one petal flap to the middle. Turn over and repeat with the opposite petal flap. Open like a book and repeat with the other two petal flaps.

9 The flower is opening! Gently fan out the main petals and curl them over a pencil. Brush with a little gold paint.

Paint a thin stick green, or use a flower wire, and push through the centre of the lily as a stem. Add a blob of sticky putty to the inside end and pull down gently so it holds the flower.

2 Angel dress

Angels are part of every nativity play. Make this simple tunic so you can be an angel.

The traditional colours for the Christmas angel in a play are white and gold.

1 Hold your arms in a T to be measured: from elbow to elbow is the width; from neck to ankle is the length. Cut two rectangles of white fabric this size. Cut two 20cm wider in tulle.

2 If the white fabric is the sort that frays, turn in the side and lower edges and stitch in place. Then centre one tulle piece on one white piece and stitch the top edges together. Repeat with the other pair.

3 Fold the top edge over by 3cm. Then fold lengthwise to find the centre and pin. Unfold and measure 5cm left and right of this point for the neck. Mark with a pin each side.

4 Now divide the shoulder fabric from side edge to centre pin into three equal sections – so you have two equally spaced pins on each shoulder. These are the pinch marks for the pleats.

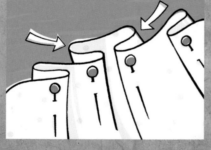

5 To make each pleat, pinch the fabric between finger and thumb at each pin in turn, and fold it towards the centre. Pin each in place pointing slightly down from the edge to make a neckline curve. Do this for the front and the back.

6 Hold the pleats in place with several stitches, or simply staple them. Hide the stitch or staple with beads or buttons.

7 Stitch a gold ribbon to each shoulder edge front and back. Tie these together to hold the tunic at the shoulders.

8 Use a safety pin or a few stitches to hold the sides overlapped at the waist. Wear another ribbon as a sash.

The sides of this tunic are left open and are easy to walk in. Wear white shorts or tights underneath.

3 Heavenly halo

An angel is said to shine with all the glory of heaven. Angels are often depicted with a halo of light.

You can make this halo to wear. Add as many glittery bits as you want to make it heavenly!

1 Draw a circle with a 15cm radius (30cm diameter) on gold card.

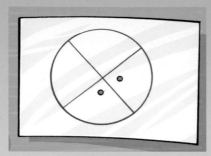

2 On one side, very lightly mark the circle into quarters as shown. Mark two holes about 3cm down from where the lines cross and 2cm to either side. Punch with a thick needle.

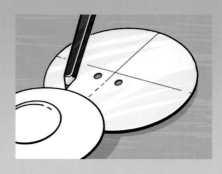

3 Next, use a small plate to cut an arc shape directly below these holes so the halo will fit comfortably against the back of your neck.

4 Meanwhile, draw a ring of silver card with an outer radius of 14cm and an inner radius of 10cm. Cut it out. Punch stars in gold card or buy giant star confetti.

5 Glue the silver ring on the gold side and then arrange the gold stars on top. Glue in place. Trim the ring to the same shape as the neck arc.

6 Measure enough gold elastic to fit round your head with a bit extra. Thread it through the two holes and knot to fit your head.

Make sure the knot stays close to the back of your head so it will not be seen. If the halo is for a play, you may want to dry-brush gold paint on the plain (back) side rather than leave it white.

4 Winged messengers

If angels live in highest heaven, they will need wings to fly to earth. Make these feathery wings, flecked with gold.

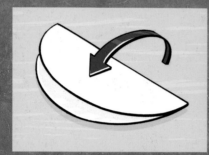

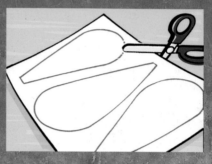

1 Draw a circle 15cm radius (30cm diameter) on white card. Cut it out and fold it in half.

2 Fold a piece of paper about 25cm x 10cm in half lengthways. Draw a half feather shape and cut it out. Unfold your feather template.

3 Use the template to outline 6 feathers on white card. Cut them out.

4 Put gesso on a saucer. Finger paint the semicircle of folded card in swirls like soft feathers. Finger paint the feather shapes with straight strokes to look like flight feathers.

5 When the gesso is nearly dry, add highlights by fingering on gold glitter glue. When one side is dry, add gesso and glitter to the other side of the feathers. Do the same with the circle if you wish.

6 Now unfold the semicircle and tape the feathers in place. Add a staple to each through the back semicircle for extra strength if you wish.

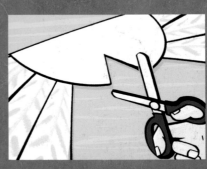

7 Fold the top semicircle down and glue. Cut a notch and staple either side.

8 Punch holes as shown and thread a loop of gold cord elastic in a figure of eight pattern, leaving a loop long enough for each arm.

5 Angel cards

An angel is a messenger, and so angel cards are the perfect way to send a Christmas message.

Begin by copying the angel shape on the back cover and cut it out of tough paper to make a reverse stencil.

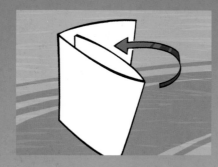  

1 Draw a rectangle of 30cm x 10cm on white card. Mark fold lines at 10cm and 20cm. Cut it out and fold.

2 Dot some glue on the skirt part of the stencil to hold it in the centre part of the card. Use a stiff stencil brush to dab paint around the outer part of the card not covered by the stencil.

3 Take off the stencil and draw your angel head and shoulders using crayons, markers or pastels.

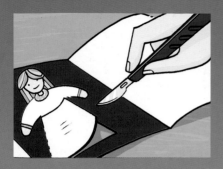

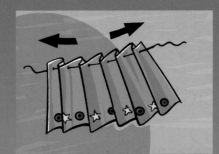

4 Ask a grown-up to help you cut out the skirt area using a craft knife on a cutting board.

5 Choose ribbon or fabric folded double along the hem for the skirt. Decorate with beads or sequins if you wish.

6 Make a line of in-and-out stitches along the top edge. Hold the thread as you squeeze the fabric into gathers.

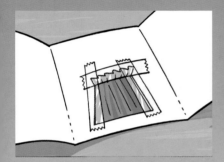

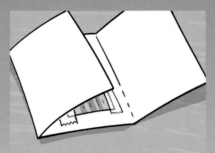

7 Tape the gathered top skirt on the underside of the card so the hem is just at the edge of the hole. Tape the sides but leave the hem free.

8 Glue the front panel in place over the wrong side of the skirt.

Add extra stars or jewels to the front of the card for a glittery effect.

6 Angel gifts

Giving gifts at Christmas makes the world feel more like heaven. So angel shapes make perfect gift wrap.

Select plain-coloured paper to print on. It should be tough enough to last and thin enough to wrap around a parcel.

1 Begin by copying the angel body and wing shapes from the back cover onto card. Cut them out to make a template. Then draw round them on a sponge.

2 Ask a grown up to help you snip the shapes out of the sponge. It won't matter if they are not perfectly even.

3 Choose the paint for the wing colour. Pour a thin layer onto a plate. Dab the wing sponge in lightly, keeping the shape flat.

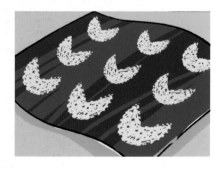

4 Blot the sponge on a scrap of paper, then print on the wrapping paper. Dab, blot and print all over the paper, leaving space for the angel body. Allow to dry.

5 Choose the paint for the body. Use the same method to print the body over the wings.

Sponge printing gives a soft, handmade effect. Have fun printing and don't worry about 'perfect' shapes.

7 Angel gift tags

Make simple tags to match your wrapping paper.
    Leave the back of the angel tags plain to write your message on.
    Begin by copying the angel body and wing shapes from the
back cover onto card. Cut them out to make templates.

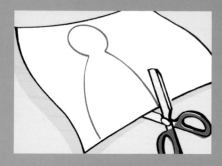

1 Draw round the angel template on white card and cut it out.

2 Colour the halo, hair, dress and cheeks with crayons or markers.

3 Draw round the wing template on metallic card. Cut it out and glue it onto the back of the angel.

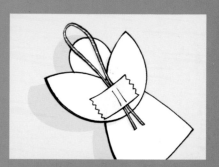

4 Tape a loop of string onto the back.

You can add lots of glittery bits to make your angels sparkle.

8 Spoon archangel

The Christmas angel, Gabriel, is sometimes described as an especially important angel – an archangel.

A wooden spoon is the framework for this angel, which is simple to make but can be decorated extravagantly.

1 Paint the spoon head all over if you wish. When it is dry, use marker pens to add the eyes, mouth and hair.

2 Lay the spoon on metallic card and draw a line close to the edge of the spoon and an outer line for the halo. Cut around the outer line. Decorate the card if you wish.

3 Put strong white glue on the rim of the spoon (not the face side) and attach the halo. It will help to lay the spoon and halo flat and weight them till the glue is dry.

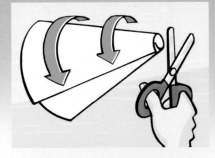

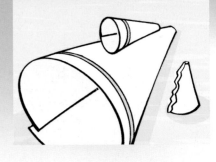

4 Measure the length of the spoon handle and add 3cm. Draw a quarter circle with this radius on the paper you have chosen for the dress.

5 Fold the paper into a cone dress. Tape the cone in place and snip the top to make an opening for the spoon handle.

6 Now cut two quarter circles a third of the radius of the dress. Fold into cones for the sleeves. Fix in place with glue or double-sided tape. Put the spoon in the dress.

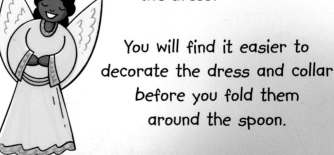

You will find it easier to decorate the dress and collar before you fold them around the spoon.

This angel stands by itself. You can use the same method make other spoon figures for a crib scene.

7 For the collar, draw a semicircle with a radius of about 6cm. Draw a smaller semicircle within that. Cut out this band. Curve it around the neck and tape in place.

9 Tree hearts

These woven hearts are quick to make, so you can make lots to hang on the tree. They look pretty as they are, or you can fill them with tiny surprises to give to guests.

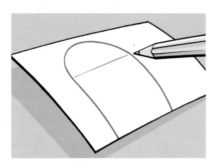

1 Draw the template. Begin with a rectangle 4.5cm x 5cm. Now add a semicircle on top of one of the shorter sides. Cut it out.

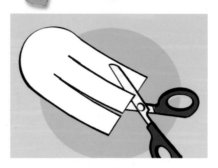

2 Mark points at 1.5cm and 3cm along the top and bottom of the rectangle part. Join the lines. Cut away the lines to leave two thin slots. Your template is like a comb.

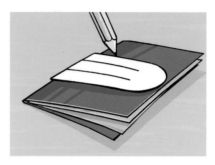

3 Take two sheets of paper at least 5cm x 15cm and fold them in half together. Place the base of the template on the fold and draw round it and up the slots.

4 Cut the two shapes out. Then cut up the lines – cutting longer rather than shorter.

5 Weave the lower strip of the right hand part into the left: insert, wrap, insert.

6 Weave the second strip of the right hand part into the left: wrap, insert, wrap.

There are so many ways to add pretty bits to these hearts. Just use your imagination!

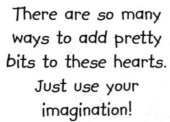

7 Weave the third strip of the right hand part into the left: insert, wrap, insert.

8 Decorate the hearts as you wish and add a hanging loop.

10 Peg angels

In the story of the nativity, the shepherds on the hillside saw multitudes of angels. These tiny peg angels for the Christmas tree wear country dresses for visiting country people. Once you've got the hang of making them, you can make lots as they only need tiny amounts of materials.

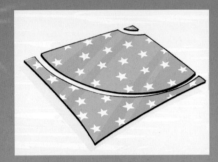

1 First cut a quarter circle of dress paper about 10cm long as shown. Cut a tiny circle for the neck.

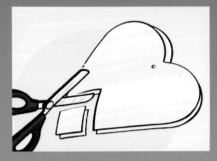

2 Now cut two heart shapes in silver card for the wings. Glue the plain sides together. Cut off the lower point as a notch and punch a hole with a large needle as shown.

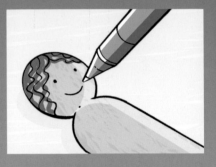

3 Next take a dolly clothes peg and use markers to draw two eyes, a mouth and curly hair.

4 Tape one edge of the dress on the peg. Wind the rest round in a cone shape and tape shut.

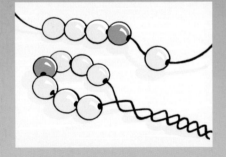

5 Now take a 40cm piece of craft wire and thread beads onto the centre. Wind into a circle halo that 'fits' the peg head and twist. Keep winding to make a stalk.

6 Now take the ends round the neck: this holds the halo in place and makes a necklace. Take the wire round to the back of the neck and twist.

To hang these angels on the tree, tie fine metallic thread around the neck and then knot the ends into a hanging loop.

7 Thread the two ends of wire through the hole in the wings and pull down to the notch.

8 Hold the wings-and-halo on the back of the angel and wind the ends of wire round the dress as a sash. Twist shut.

11 Table angels

These angels sit prettily on the Christmas table to tell people where to sit. Write the name of each person on 'their' angel. Hide sweets or a surprise gift under the skirts.

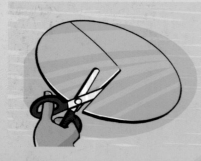

1 Draw a circle with a 10cm radius on coloured card. Mark a pie slice that is one third of the whole and cut it out. This third makes the angel.

2 Decorate the outer edge of the circle as the hem of the angel dress, then wrap into a cone and tape in place.

3 Cut a piece of white paper in half for the angel's wings and cut a spoon shape, taking care not to make the folded part too narrow. Unfold and edge with gold marker. Glue to the back of the cone, at the join.

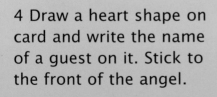

4 Draw a heart shape on card and write the name of a guest on it. Stick to the front of the angel.

5 Using white card, draw round a coin for the angel head and then add a long neck. Cut out and draw the face.

6 Snip the top of the dress cone so you can insert the neck. Once you have got it in the right position, tape it in place on the inside and bend it so the angel smiles at your guest.

12 Gingerbread angels

Angels that are good enough to eat!
 Wash your hands before you do any cooking. Ask a grown-up to help, and let them deal with the oven and its controls.

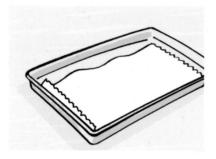

1 Preheat the oven to 170°C. Choose a baking tray and line it with baking parchment.

2 Sieve into a bowl 325g plain flour, 1 teaspoon of bicarbonate of soda and 2 teaspoons of ground ginger. Mix.

3 Place in a saucepan 125g butter, 100g brown sugar, 3 tablespoons of golden syrup and 1 tablespoon of black treacle. Put on the stove on a low heat so the butter melts. Stir together.

4 Pour the melted ingredients into the bowl of dry ingredients and mix into a ball of dough. Chill for an hour.

5 Put baking parchment on a work surface and dust with flour. Use a rolling pin to roll the dough into a sheet about 5mm thick, using extra flour to stop it sticking.

6 Use an angel cutter and lift the shapes with a broad palette knife onto the lined baking tray. Leave room between each. Bake for 9–10 minutes till just going brown. Allow to cool.

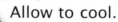

7 Decorate with royal icing from a writing nozzle and let it set.

8 Add a ribbon sash and tie the bow to look like wings.

13 Cloud coconut macaroons

These little treats look like clouds and taste heavenly! Present them in a light-as-air package.

Wash your hands before you do any cooking. Ask a grown-up to help, and let them deal with the oven and its controls.

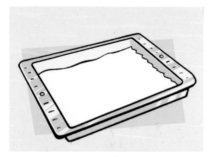

1 Preheat the oven to 150°C. Choose a baking tray and line it with baking parchment.

2 Ask a grown-up to help you put two egg whites in a bowl, and beat with an electric whisk till white and fluffy.

3 Gradually add 170g sugar, pausing the whisk each time you add a spoonful. Beat for 3 minutes.

4 Gently stir in 180g dessicated coconut and 100g chopped macadamia nuts.

5 Use a spoon to make little heaps of mix on the baking tray. Bake for 10–12 minutes. Leave to cool.

6 Cut rectangles of cellophane about 40cm x 30cm. Tape as shown along the shorter side.

7 Next, gather one end and spread the gathers evenly. Tape tightly shut and trim the 'stalk'.

8 Turn the bag over and add 4–5 macaroons. Tie with a ribbon of cellophane.

14 Starry gifts

Into the story of Jesus' birth come wise men bearing gifts, a bright shining star leading the way to Bethlehem, and then angels guiding the travellers home…

 Wrap a small gift in tissue paper before presenting it in one of these glamorously Christmassy boxes.

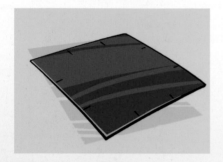

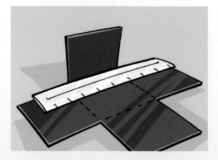

1 Begin with a square of card 30cm x 30cm. Mark 10cm and 20cm along each edge.

2 Draw the joining lines with a ruler and cut out the corners to leave a cross shape.

3 Fold up the sides of the box, laying a ruler along the line you drew to make a good edge.

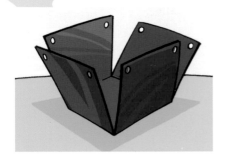

4 Mark holes in each upper corner of the sides and punch a hole.

5 Cut eight (or more!) star shapes out of metallic card (or use a star punch). Use a thick needle to punch a pair of holes in each to make a 'button'.

6 Cut a piece of beading wire 10cm long. Thread it up one hole in a star button, add some tiny beads, then take the wire down the other hole. Centre the button and twist the wire.

As your skill grows, you can use wire and ever more stars and beads.

7 Now thread the decorated wire through two corner holes to hold them together. Twist in place. Do the same for all the corners.

8 Now cut a longer piece of wire at least 20cm long and thread star buttons and beads onto it. Twist to attach it in an arch from one corner hole to another.

15 Hearts with love from...

Send a heart-shaped letter: to invite someone, to tell your news, to say thank you.

1 Take a piece of paper 20cm x 20cm. Fold it in half and lightly draw half a heart. Cut it out and unfold the heart.

2 Take a piece of soft tissue paper and fold it in half. Draw a heart a little smaller all around than the first heart.

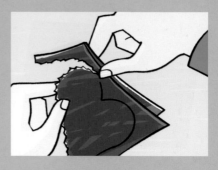

3 Cut it out or, for a soft finish, tear it bit by bit, holding the paper close between finger and thumb to prevent wild tears.

4 Glue the inner heart to the outer heart. Now fold the top curves down, the sides to the middle, and the lower point up like an envelope.

5 Unfold the heart to write your message. Then refold and seal with a dab of glue or a star sticker.

There are many different ways to give the outer paper the angel touch, with gold and glitter as you fancy.

16 Just a glimpse

Do angels only belong at Christmas… or might you catch a glimpse of heaven at any time when there is love and kindness?

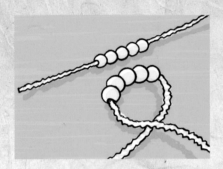

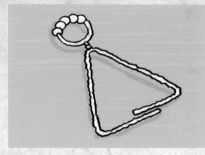

1 Thread a few beads onto the mid point of a gold or silver plush wire. Bend the wire down into a hairpin shape and then twist the top to make a 'head'.

2 Bend the remaining ends into a triangle shape for the skirt. Twist the ends along the lower edge to hold the shape.

3 Take a contrasting plush wire and bend up from the centre into a hairpin shape. Then wind the ends down to make two ovals (a pretzel shape). Twist the ovals so they hold their shape as wings.

4 Wind the remaining ends of this wire around the angel to hold the wings in place and make a 'body'. Add a hanging loop from the head if you wish.